A Case for The Presidential Draft

A Radical New Approach to

How We Select & Elect Our Leaders

By

Jack Thomas

Table of Contents

Prologue:

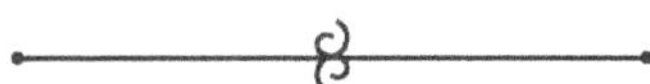

Get ready, because we're about to dive deep into the fascinating world of American politics! Specifically, we'll take a close look at how we can improve the process of selecting and electing the president, vice president, and cabinet members—in other words, the nation's top leadership.

As things stand, the system we use to elect our President in the USA is about as reliable as a GPS in a remote jungle. No signal. Doesn't work and cannot be fixed.

It's broken, my friends.

And because it's broken, we are not getting candidates that are the best that the US has to offer. Our voting system is not without its flaws and needs to be urgently revamped before things get worse. That is not to say that there is some other "perfect" election process somewhere else in the world that we can mimic. Currently, there is no other system that is seemingly perfect.

It seems that it is time to open a discussion about how to reinvent the process. The current process was set up over 200 years ago, and a lot has changed since then.

Back in the good old days, our political leaders were like a team of superheroes. These individuals truly represented their states. They didn't just follow party lines; they were loyal to their constituents and ideals. They actually did what they promised...yes shocking, I know!

In the past, becoming a political star was akin to climbing Everest – you worked your tail off, showed exemplary leadership, and amassed a wealth of real-world experience. Only then did you throw your hat into the political ring, bringing with your real-world experience. These citizens formed a rich tapestry of backgrounds, from military veterans to business moguls to teachers to thespians. They didn't just govern; they orchestrated a symphony of diverse perspectives for the betterment of the nations. They were less concerned about toeing the party line and more about doing right by their people, embodying loyalty to constituents over party politics.

But, in modern times, even those who aim to scale Mount Everest are quite often unprepared and not experienced enough. Because of that, at the crest, even the most experienced climbers must wait through long lines of amateurs vying for a peak that they are not worthy of obtaining. Those who have the experience and the know-how have to endure these dreadful lines packed with appalling, immature people to try to get to the top. And those armatures can completely turn any situation into a life-or-death struggle should the weather turn bad.

Talk about a perfect metaphor!

But returning to the current political scene, we are also inundated with armatures. Now, anyone with a pulse and a Political Science degree thinks they can play in the big leagues. It's like a scene out of "The Twilight Zone". Experience? Who needs it? A solid Resume? I'll make it up or at least enhance it. Nowadays, it seems like politicians are elected based on their catchy campaign slogans rather than any meaningful ideals. And once they've won that coveted seat in office, it's like they have collective amnesia about the pledges they made to get there.

Many of these contenders lack the real-world experience to understand life beyond the political bubble – a kind of fantasy world where fairies, leprechauns, and elves probably vote too (be wary, they may be on the voter lists as an underrepresented segment of our population).

Now, it's not uncommon for fresh-faced, idealistic young people to major in Political Science, dip their toes into internships or community leadership roles, and then lead headfirst into the political fray before they've had a job outside the political arena. They are completely out of touch with the struggles, dreams, and necessities of the families, older people, and the general public who are not within their same socioeconomic class.

And let's talk about their unrealistic ideals. When we're in our teens and twenties, we all believe in rainbows, unicorns, miracles, and a world where everyone shares happily ever after. These young politicians believe in idealistic paradigms, such as socialism and communism, and tend to overlook the pragmatic constraints intrinsic to sociopolitical systems.

It takes some hard knocks and a few "adulting" years to realize life's not a utopian picnic. As it turns out, we're not all equal contributors, and some people want a free ride on the train.

As with any group of people, the 80/20 rule kicks in – 20% of the people do 80% of the work, while the other 80% complain about life being unfair. It's like a sitcom where the hard-working characters are disillusioned with the lazy, complaining personas, and you begin to wonder why they're still hanging out together.

To make matters worse, the political climate has become so toxic that even the brightest and most experienced people are steering clear of the political arena, treating it like a plague of locusts. Why would anyone choose to be a politician when the private sector offers better pay, less stress, and far less scrutiny?

Now, sticking with the old model is like insisting on using a cassette player in the age of streaming. It's outdated; the tapes are most likely corrupted and inefficient.

We need a new way, and I'm about to drop some crazy ideas. Fingers crossed that some very brave and smart individuals can take these minuscule ideas and turn them into something fair, coherent, and, most importantly, doable.

This is my little drop of water to contribute to an ocean of change. Thanks for being here to ride this crazy wave with me!

While I have been quite whimsical and satirical in this prologue, the political polarization in the US and the world is a growing problem. All jokes aside, I think we need to mix the red and the blue ideologies, and with a bit of humor, we can find common ground and agree to disagree about our differences.

The rest of this book is not written in such a satirical fashion, but I may try to interject some humorous parts to keep it light.

As always, thanks for taking the time to read my little book!

P.S. For anyone interested in reviewing how we arrived at this point, there is a very brief summary of the history of democracy in the appendix. I emphasize "very brief" because the subject is filled with countless twists, turns, side notes, and anecdotes at every stage—covering the full history of democracy would be nearly impossible.

Chapter I:

Who Would Ever Want to be King?

The Reluctant Leader's Plight

Ever stop to wonder who in their right mind would willingly sign up for the daunting task of being the President of the United States? It is really a bit of a head-scratcher. The top of the top, the best and brightest among us, seem to eye the Oval Office with the same enthusiasm one might reserve for a colonoscopy. And can you blame them?

Let's break down why. The pay is nothing compared to the Herculean tasks at hand; the odds of success are slim, and the stakes? Well, let's say they're higher than a kite in a hurricane. Little wonder that the best and brightest minds in business – the very leaders who could potentially steer this ship of the country towards smoother waters – aren't exactly lining up around the block to throw their hats into the political ring.

If you think about it, when you become president, you lose your freedom to a security detail 24/7. The Secret Service looks like your personal babysitters, they are ever-present and watching your every move. You can say goodbye to spontaneous coffee runs or strolls down Main Street – from here on out; your every move is scrutinized. You get criticized for what you say, what you wear, and even to whom you speak. Anything and everything you do will alienate some part of the population.

And then there's the legislative labyrinth you're expected to navigate. America's more divided than a bottle of water and oil, therefore taking a stance – any stance – is like stepping into a lion's den. The slightest deviation from the party line earns you a backlash of vicious rhetoric and venomous diatribes.

So, where did all this polarizing opposition come from, you ask? Some people point their fingers at the usual suspects – the secret cabal pulling the strings behind the scenes. But let's not forget the role played by our politicians themselves, stoking the fires of extremism to keep their stars shining bright.

And don't even get me started on the media. They're like the kid who won't stop poking the hornet's nest, riling folks up for the sheer thrill of watching the chaos unfold and cashing in on high ratings when it does.

But fear not because there's a glimmer of hope. The first step to fixing something is realizing that it is broken. Our system for selecting our leaders is broken. We need leaders who can bridge the gap, not widen the chasm between us. They are out there right now – they are running businesses, tilling the soil, shaping young minds, participating in podcasts and even spinning tales on the silver screen. But the thought of wading through the murky waters of politics? It's not exactly their idea of a good time.

So, what if we flipped the script? What if we ditched the tired old party primaries, slashed the obscene campaign budgets, and charted a new course toward a more inclusive, efficient way of choosing our leaders?

Picture this: a slate of 5 to 12 candidates, handpicked by the people, for the people, regardless of party affiliation or personal ambition. They're conscripted into service and tasked with running the executive branch for the next four years. No more endless committee approvals, no more wasteful spending on campaign ads – just a straightforward vote to decide who's in and who's out.

I know what you're thinking – it's a radical departure from the status quo. But hear me out. History is no stranger to seismic shifts – and we have already evolved in the past from monarchies and dictatorships to modern democracies. There are times of revolution when the winds of change have blown stronger than a hurricane.

Changing the way we select and elect our president won't be a walk in the park. But it's a small price to pay for a system that's fairer, more efficient, and, dare I say it, downright civilized. So, let's roll up our sleeves and get to work – because the future of democracy is counting on us.

Chapter II:

The History of the Draft and Conscription: From Ancient Armies to Modern Mandates

The draft, also known as conscription, is hardly a new concept. It's been around in various forms since ancient times. Societies have long grappled with the need to muster enough people to serve in their armies, especially during times of war. In ancient Greece and Rome, citizens were often required to take up arms in defense of their city-states. They truly had no choice as the alternative was that their city-state would be invaded, and they and their family may become slaves of the invaders.

Moving forward to the Middle Ages, conscription took on more formalized structures. There were times when all men aged 15-60 were called upon to defend their realm. Kings and noblemen could call upon their subjects to provide men for military service, a practice that became more organized as kingdoms and nation-states emerged. By the time of the Napoleonic Wars in the late 18th century, conscription had evolved into a highly efficient system that allowed France to field one of the largest armies Europe had ever seen—though not without controversy or resistance.

In the United States, the draft has a more modern yet equally complex history. The first significant use of conscription came during the Civil War when both the Union and the Confederacy implemented drafts to bolster their forces. The First Confederate Conscription Act made any white male between 18 and 35 years old liable to three years of military service. The second, in 1862, extended the age limit to 45 years. In 1864, they passed the third, which increased the age range from 17 to 50 years old for service of an unlimited period.

In the Union states, the first draft was established in 1863 and required registration by every male citizen between the ages of 20 and 45. People criticized the law because all those who could pay an exemption for a $300 fee could avoid the draft. Many critics argued that the law was unfair to people with low incomes.

This led to widespread dissent, including draft riots in New York City in 1863. It was a divisive issue then, and it remained so during World War I and II, the Korean War, and especially the Vietnam War, where the draft became the spark that started the fire of broader social and political unrest.

Today, the draft has largely faded from public consciousness, especially since the US moved to an all-volunteer military force in the 1970s. However, the Selective Service System still exists, and all male citizens and residents are required to register at 18, keeping the door open for conscription in the event of a national emergency.

But here's the thing: while military drafts are seen as necessary evils during times of existential threat, they are also a powerful reminder that sometimes the needs of the many outweigh the preferences of the few. It's this very principle that opens the door to a bold new idea: a presidential draft.

A Presidential Draft: The Ethics of Obligatory Leadership

The idea of obliging someone to serve as president might sound strange, even dystopian, at first glance. After all, who wants to be forced into the highest office in the land, tasked with steering the country through the myriad challenges of modern governance? But let's unpack this idea because, much like jury duty, a presidential draft could offer a way to refocus our politics on service rather than ambition.

In a democracy, we cherish the idea that our leaders are chosen by the people, for the people. But over time, this ideal has often been overshadowed by the realities of political campaigning, where candidates spend more time raising money, making promises, and strategizing for their next election than they do actually governing. It's a system that rewards charisma and connections, often at the expense of competence and integrity.

Imagine a different scenario: instead of a drawn-out election season full of campaign ads, debates, and rallies, a presidential draft pulls from a pool of qualified individuals— a draft where the 'draftees' are individuals who meet a set of stringent qualifications based on experience, knowledge, and ability to lead. This would be akin to how we draft citizens for jury duty. The core idea is simple: just as we call upon our citizens to ensure fair trials, why not call upon them to lead the nation when it's their turn?

Why a Presidential Draft Could Be Ethical

1. Shared Civic Duty: We already ask citizens to serve on juries and, in extreme cases, to fight for their country. Serving as president would be another form of civic duty—arguably the ultimate form. Just as jurors play a crucial role in upholding justice, a drafted president would be tasked with upholding democracy itself. The presidency would no longer be a personal ambition but a duty, like serving on the front lines or in a courtroom.

2. Neutralizing Ambition: One of the biggest ethical concerns with current presidential candidates is that they often pursue office out of personal ambition rather than a genuine desire to serve. A draft would cut through this problem entirely by removing the element of choice. This isn't about seeking power; it's about answering a call. The focus shifts from personal gain to public service, ensuring that the person in the role is there because the country needs them, not because they crave the spotlight.

3. Promoting Competence Over Popularity: In our current system, the race for the presidency can feel more like a popularity contest than a serious job application for one of the most demanding roles in the world. A draft would prioritize qualifications over charm and knowledge over notoriety. The pool of potential draftees could include successful governors, seasoned diplomats, business leaders, judges, professors, and others who have

demonstrated the skills and judgment necessary to lead at the highest level.

4. Balancing the Power Dynamics: The presidency, as it stands, is often swayed by partisan politics, special interest groups, and the relentless need for fundraising. A presidential draft would diminish the outsized influence of money and power in our political system. By rotating leadership through a broader segment of the populace, we could ensure a more balanced and less partisan approach to governance.

5. Temporary Obligation with Lasting Impact: Serving as president under a draft system would not be a lifetime commitment—it's a four-year term, after which the draftee can return to private life. This mirrors how we treat other civic obligations, such as jury duty or military service. It's a significant commitment, but it's also a temporary one, and it's undertaken with the understanding that it serves the greater good.

Drawing Parallels to Jury Duty

Think of it this way: no one particularly enjoys being called for jury duty. It's time-consuming, often inconvenient, and, let's be honest—it doesn't pay well. Yet we do it because we recognize that a fair trial is a cornerstone of our justice system. Serving on a jury isn't about the individual; it's about upholding a system that benefits everyone.

A presidential draft operates on the same principle. The role of the president is too important to be left solely to those who actively seek it, especially when their motivations might not always align with the public interest. By drafting qualified leaders, we could ensure that the office is filled by someone capable, dedicated, and, most importantly, obligated to serve without ulterior motives.

This system wouldn't be perfect, and it would undoubtedly face challenges—from legal questions about compulsory service to public pushback against the loss of the traditional electoral process. But as we grapple with a political landscape that often feels more like theater than governance, a presidential draft could represent a bold step towards a more ethical, equitable, and effective system of leadership.

After all, if we trust our fellow citizens to judge a defendant's guilt or innocence and to fight on the front lines in times of war, why not trust them to lead the nation when the call comes? It's not just about finding the right leader; it's about rediscovering the true spirit of public service. And in a time when that spirit often seems in short supply, maybe a presidential draft is exactly what we need to rekindle it.

Chapter III:

The Age-Old Art of Buying Votes:

From Caesar to Modern Politics

Buying votes is as old as democracy itself. In the days of Julius Caesar, politicians didn't just campaign with grand speeches and promises—they wielded a playbook of tactics designed to sway the electorate by any means necessary. And guess what? A lot of those methods haven't really gone away. They've just evolved, taken on new guises, and slipped into the modern political landscape, sometimes so seamlessly that we don't even notice.

The ancient Roman handbook included all the classics: making hollow promises that catered to voters' economic desires, bribing with cash, and promising personal favors. Today, the art of vote-buying has become more sophisticated, but the core principle remains the same: winning elections often come down to who can best offer a tangible "what's in it for me" to the voter.

The Modern Mechanics of Vote Buying

Fast forward to today, and vote-buying has evolved into more sophisticated forms. It's no longer just shady backroom deals with envelopes of cash (though that still occurs in some places). Modern tactics are often subtler but just as manipulative. Political strategists carefully analyze what has worked in other countries and adapt these methods to suit their candidates' platforms, with little regard for ethics. After all, they argue, if the end result is getting their candidate—the one who will supposedly do the most good—into power, isn't it justified?

These are some of the top ways votes are being bought around the world today:

Direct Buyouts:

- Cash payments

- Gifts like food, clothing, or other goods

- Threats, intimidation, and coercion

- Conditional cash transfers

- Vote pledges or outright vote-selling

Indirect Vote Buying:

- Forgiving student loans

- Offering paths to citizenship (e.g., fast-tracking immigration processes)

- Raising the minimum wage or reducing work hours

- Expanding unemployment benefits

- Promising direct government payments or financial relief

- Offering jobs or government positions in exchange for votes

- Delivering public services or development projects targeted to specific communities

- Reducing personal debts or offering public housing to voters

Indirect methods are especially widespread in U.S. politics. While they may not be as blatantly transactional as handing over cash, they achieve the same goal: votes in exchange for benefits. These strategies often target vulnerable or less informed voters who may not realize that these "free" perks are funded by taxpayers—including themselves. In some cases, the very aid intended to help them can end up holding them back, leading to increased tax burdens or disincentives to pursue further education or career advancement.

The Slippery Slope to Systemic Problems

While it's easy to sympathize with the idea of helping those in tough situations, these practices raise a thorny question: At what point does benevolence cross the line into manipulation? If left unchecked, these forms of vote-buying can gradually erode the foundations of democracy, nudging it towards something resembling a welfare state where power hinges on who can promise the most to the most people rather than on who can lead effectively or fairly.

The risk isn't just hypothetical. History offers countless examples of what happens when social safety nets are exploited as tools of political power. The argument that this could steer the country towards socialism or even communism isn't just fearmongering; it's based on patterns we've seen before. Remember "Animal Farm"? A revolution for the common good can quickly turn into a system where the pigs are back at the trough, just with a different set of rules.

Is There a Solution?

So, how do we keep our social safety nets without turning them into weapons of vote-buying? One radical proposal is to suspend the voting rights of those who receive certain government benefits, at least temporarily. The logic goes like this: if recipients of these benefits can't vote while they're receiving aid, politicians have less incentive to buy their loyalty with promises of more aid. This would theoretically shift the focus back to policies that benefit society as a whole, rather than just a segment of voters who the promise of financial relief can sway.

But let's pause here for a reality check. Proposing to disenfranchise a section of the population—even temporarily—is a drastic measure, and it's fraught with ethical and legal complications. The idea of stripping voting rights based on socioeconomic status or dependency on government aid could be viewed as undemocratic and regressive. And besides, the pendulum of US politics already swings predictably between the two main parties every eight years or so, as seen in recent history:

- Ronald Reagan (1981-1989) - 8 years, Republican

- George H. W. Bush (1989-1993) - 4 years, Republican

- Bill Clinton (1993-2001) - 8 years, Democrat

- George W. Bush (2001-2009) - 8 years, Republican

- Barack Obama (2009-2017) - 8 years, Democrat

- Donald Trump (2017-2021) - 4 years, Republican

- Joe Biden (2021-present) - Democrat

To truly curb the influence of vote-buying, a more systemic change might be needed—something like a presidential draft, which would pull candidates from a pool of qualified individuals regardless of party affiliation or campaign promises. In this scenario, candidates might be less likely to offer vote-buying schemes because their tenure in office wouldn't hinge on courting voters with promises of cash or benefits.

Imagine the fallout of such a system during times of widespread government aid, like the pandemic stimulus checks. If the electorate knows that the person in office is there due to a draft rather than a campaign built on promises of financial relief, there could be less motivation for policymakers to use public funds as bait.

The Fiscal Cliff

And let's not overlook the looming fiscal cliff we're all edging toward. The national debt has surged past $35 trillion—a figure so staggering that it feels abstract to the average person. But the reality is that this debt, and the interest it accrues, will burden future generations unless we find the courage—and political will—to stop kicking the can down the road.

This isn't just a political issue; it's a societal one. It's about confronting the uncomfortable truths about our collective spending habits and acknowledging the long-term consequences of short-term vote-buying schemes. Addressing this problem will require more than policy tweaks or flashy new ideas—it demands a fundamental rethinking of how we choose our leaders and what we expect from them.

The bottom line is that while vote-buying, in all its forms, might seem like a necessary evil or just part of the political game, it comes with very real costs. And those costs are borne by **YOU**, the taxpayer—not only in dollars but in the erosion of democratic principles and the integrity of the systems designed to serve us all, not just the highest bidder.

Chapter IV:

The Hidden Reality of Voter Fraud: Separating Myth from Fact

Contrary to the comforting belief held by many, voter fraud does happen. It might not be the widespread epidemic some alarmists claim, but it's real enough to merit our attention. As a society, if we value the integrity of our democratic process, we need to be vigilant and proactive in rooting out all types of voter fraud, no matter how small or infrequent. After all, even the tiniest crack in the foundation can eventually bring down a house.

Most of us would never dream of committing voter fraud; it's simply not in our nature. But it's a mistake to assume that everyone shares this same moral compass. For some, the mantra "the ends justify the means" reigns supreme, and they'll bend or break the rules if it means securing a win for their preferred candidate.

The Challenge of Catching Every Culprit

So, how do we put an end to voter fraud? First, let's acknowledge the reality: eradicating every instance of voter fraud is like trying to stop every raindrop in a storm. Small-scale fraud—like someone walking into a polling place posing as their grandmother—might go unnoticed. But with the right tools and systems, we can at least close the gaps that allow the most egregious abuses to occur.

For example, cases of people voting on behalf of their deceased relatives could be minimized with a national database of eligible voters that's updated in real-time. This database would track not only who is eligible to vote but also who is temporarily or permanently ineligible. A voter registration card system, similar to a driver's license with photo identification and an embedded chip, could ensure that once a vote is cast, it's recorded and can't be duplicated. This could prevent the dead from voting, curb double voting, and put a stop to other common forms of fraud.

Leveraging Technology for Secure Voting

Another innovative approach could be to utilize blockchain technology—a digital public ledger that's virtually impossible to alter. Votes could be recorded using unique voter identification numbers (instead of names) to maintain anonymity while providing a transparent and secure record of every vote cast. This would create a system that's both open to public scrutiny and impervious to tampering, a far cry from the opaque systems we currently rely on.

But let's not kid ourselves: technology isn't a cure-all. It's a tool, and like any tool, it can be misused. To effectively combat voter fraud, we need to target the areas where fraud is most likely to occur:

Key Vulnerabilities in the Voting Process:

- **Mail-in Votes:** These are convenient but can be susceptible to manipulation. Implementing strict time limits and tracking mechanisms can help ensure that every vote is legitimate and accounted for.

- **Data Entry Points:** This is where tallied votes are entered into the central system. Mistakes, intentional or not, can skew results, so this stage needs ironclad oversight.

- **Vote Tabulation Algorithms:** Computer systems that count votes are another potential weak spot. A flawed algorithm, whether by design or by error, could dramatically alter outcomes.

Keeping the Counters Honest

One of the simplest yet most overlooked safeguards is to ensure no single company holds the keys to the entire electoral process. Allowing one company to create, implement, and run the software systems for elections is like asking a fox to guard the henhouse. It's just not common sense. Instead, the task of tallying votes should be divided among at least three independent American companies, each working in isolation. Their results should be compared and contrasted, ensuring that discrepancies are caught and investigated.

Yes, this approach is more expensive, but democracy has never been about taking the cheapest route. Accuracy and trustworthiness come at a price, and when it comes to something as crucial as our electoral process, cutting corners isn't an option.

In Conclusion

The fight against voter fraud isn't about vilifying one side or the other—it's about protecting the foundation of democracy: the guarantee that every vote counts and each election reflects the true will of the people. While it's unrealistic to catch every instance of fraud, we can take meaningful steps to make it much harder for those seeking to undermine the system. By embracing technology, strengthening controls at vulnerable points, and distributing the responsibility for counting votes, we can create a more secure and resilient voting process.

If we fail to take these steps, we risk eroding the public trust that keeps our democracy functioning. Without that trust, democracy becomes just a shadow of what it's meant to be.

As the Roman poet Juvenal asked, "Who will guard the guards themselves?" This question is as relevant today as ever. It serves as a reminder that even those entrusted with protecting the system require oversight, demanding our constant attention and vigilance.

Chapter V:

The Two-Party System in the US:

Who Really Benefits?

The two-party system in the United States, dominated by the Republicans and Democrats, offers some clear benefits to politicians and the political machinery, but is it truly serving the best interests of the public? On the surface, the system provides simplicity at the ballot box—just two main choices. However, as society has evolved, so have voters, and many are now questioning whether limiting choices to just two parties still makes sense in a diverse and complex nation. In reality, the two-party system seems designed to benefit politicians more than the people they represent.

Politicians affiliated with one of the two major parties enjoy a host of advantages: access to extensive resources, established voter networks, instant recognition, and the credibility that comes from aligning with a familiar brand. Most importantly, they gain significant fundraising power, access to data analytics, advertising channels, and a pool of experienced campaign staff—all of which reduce the individual costs and risks of running for office.

But let's dig deeper: while these perks are great for the candidates, is this two-party stranglehold good for the country? To answer that, let's explore the benefits and drawbacks of the two-party system.

Benefits of the Two-Party System

1. **Stability and Governability:**

   - **Predictable Transitions:** With only two major parties, government transitions are more predictable and orderly, which can help maintain political stability.

   - **Efficient Governance:** Fewer parties mean simpler government formation, avoiding the messiness of coalition-building that plagues multi-party systems.

2. **Clear Accountability:**

   - **Responsibility:** With just two parties, it's easier for voters to hold one accountable for policy outcomes, making the lines of responsibility clear.

   - **Focused Debates:** Political debates tend to concentrate on the major issues of the day rather than being diluted across a plethora of minor party concerns.

3. **Policy Continuity:**

   - **Long-term Planning:** Major parties often have more consistent policy platforms, allowing for more continuity and strategic planning over time.

- o **Strategic Governance:** Dominant parties are usually equipped to create comprehensive policy agendas, leading to more cohesive governance.

4. **Simplified Voting Process:**

- o **Ease of Choice:** The system simplifies voting by reducing the number of choices, making it easier for voters to decide.

- o **Reduced Ballot Confusion:** Fewer candidates on the ballot reduce confusion, which can make the voting process more straightforward.

5. **Moderation of Extremes:**

- o **Centrism:** Major parties, needing to appeal to a broad voter base, often gravitate towards moderate positions, which can promote social cohesion.

- o **Broad Coalitions:** Both parties must build diverse coalitions to win, encouraging compromise and inclusive policies.

These benefits illustrate how the two-party system can help maintain stability and clarity in governance. However, it's not without significant drawbacks, which can impact voter representation and the overall health of democracy.

Drawbacks of the Two-Party System

1. **Limited Representation:**

   - **Narrow Choices:** The two-party system often forces voters into a binary choice, sidelining a range of other political viewpoints.

   - **Marginalization of Minorities:** Smaller parties and minority interests struggle for representation in a system dominated by two major players.

2. **Polarization:**

   - **Partisan Divisions:** With only two dominant parties, the political landscape can become deeply polarized, leading to legislative gridlock.

   - **Us vs. Them Mentality:** The rivalry between the two parties can foster a toxic, adversarial culture that stifles cooperation.

3. **Suppression of Third Parties:**

   - **Barriers to Entry:** Third-party candidates face significant obstacles, from stringent ballot access laws to exclusion from major debates.

   - **Wasted Vote Syndrome:** Fear of wasting votes keeps many from supporting third-party candidates, reinforcing the dominance of the major parties.

4. **Policy Stagnation:**

   o **Lack of Innovation:** With only two major voices, innovative policies and new ideas often take a backseat to party loyalty and status quo politics.

   o **Entrenchment of Power:** The established parties can become complacent, leading to resistance to necessary reforms and entrenchment of political power.

5. **Voter Disenfranchisement:**

   o **Disillusionment:** Voters who don't align with either major party may feel excluded from the political process, reducing overall engagement and turnout.

   o **Overlooked Issues:** Key issues that don't fit neatly into the major party platforms often go unaddressed, leaving significant portions of the electorate without representation.

6. **Negative Campaigning:**

   o **Attack Politics:** The fierce competition between the two parties often leads to negative campaigning, which can create a hostile political environment and discourage voter participation.

   o **Focus on Winning Over Governing:** The emphasis on defeating the opposing party can overshadow the actual work of effective governance.

7. **Influence of Special Interests:**

   o **Dependency on Donors:** Both major parties rely heavily on large donors, which can skew policies in favor of special interest groups over the public good.

   o **Lobbying Power:** Special interests and lobbyists wield significant influence in a two-party system, often driving policy decisions.

8. **Gridlock and Inefficiency:**

   o **Legislative Stalemate:** Deep divisions between the two parties can lead to frequent gridlock, slowing down or halting legislative progress on critical issues.

   o **Slow Response:** Partisan battles often delay responses to emerging challenges, prioritizing political gain over effective action.

What If We Did Away with Party Affiliation?

Imagine a political landscape where party affiliations were prohibited, and each candidate had to run purely on their merit. How would this reshape our democracy, and could it help to mitigate some of the issues we see with the current system?

Potential Impacts of a Non-Partisan Political System

1. **Candidate Diversity and Representation:**

   - **Increased Diversity:** Without parties, we might see a wider array of candidates with diverse ideas and backgrounds, reflecting the true breadth of public opinion.

   - **Focus on Individual Merit:** Candidates would need to win voters over based on their qualifications, character, and policies rather than relying on party branding.

2. **Campaign Financing and Donation Fraud:**

   - **Reduced Influence of Major Donors:** Without parties, there would be less emphasis on large-scale funding, potentially diminishing the sway of special interests.

   - **More Transparent Funding:** Campaigns might rely more on small donations from individuals, increasing transparency and reducing opportunities for financial misconduct.

3. **Legislation and Governance:**

   - **Collaboration over Partisanship:** With no party lines to divide them, legislators might collaborate more freely, focusing on issue-based alliances and pragmatic solutions.

   - **Focus on Constituents:** Elected officials would likely prioritize their constituents' needs over party agendas, leading to more responsive and representative governance.

4. **Reduction in Polarization:**

   o **Less of Us vs. Them:** The absence of party labels could reduce the binary opposition that drives much of today's political polarization, encouraging a more nuanced and inclusive dialogue.

   o **Encouragement of Moderation:** Candidates would need to appeal to a broader electorate, fostering more centrist and widely acceptable policies.

Potential Benefits

1. **Enhanced Accountability:**

   o **Direct Accountability:** Without party shields, voters could hold each candidate directly accountable for their actions and promises.

   o **Personal Responsibility:** Politicians would stand on their records, increasing personal accountability and reducing the ability to deflect blame onto a party.

2. **Innovation in Policy:**

   o **New Ideas:** A broader range of candidates could bring fresh perspectives and innovative solutions to the table, driving a more dynamic political discourse.

- o **Dynamic Problem-Solving:** With legislators free from party constraints, the legislative process could become more adaptable and responsive to changing needs.

3. **Voter Engagement and Participation:**

   - o **Informed Voting:** Without parties to rely on, voters might become more engaged and informed, making decisions based on the actual merits of the candidates.

   - o **Increased Participation:** A more diverse and representative field of candidates could attract a wider range of voters, boosting overall civic participation.

Challenges and Considerations

While the potential benefits of a non-partisan system are significant, there are also challenges to consider:

1. **Campaign Costs:**

   - o **Individual Burden:** Candidates would need to fund their campaigns, potentially disadvantaging those without significant resources or fundraising networks.

   - o **Resource Allocation:** Ensuring fair access to media and other campaign resources would be crucial to maintaining equity among candidates.

2. **Legislative Coordination:**

   - **Organizing Votes:** Without party structures, coordinating votes and ensuring legislative coherence could be more complex.

   - **Leadership Roles:** New mechanisms would be needed to define and elect leadership within a non-partisan legislature.

3. **Public Adaptation:**

   - **Voter Education:** Shifting to a non-partisan system would require significant voter education to help the public adapt and evaluate candidates on individual merits.

   - **Cultural Shift:** Moving away from deeply entrenched party loyalties would take time and concerted effort.

Transitioning to a system without party affiliations could foster a more merit-based, accountable, and less polarized political environment. While it would bring benefits like reducing donor influence, enhancing collaboration, and encouraging innovation, it would also pose challenges related to campaign financing, legislative coordination, and public adaptation. But in a time when the public's faith in political institutions is waning, perhaps it's a change worth considering. After all, democracy thrives on the strength of its ideas, not the color of its banners.

Chapter VI:

Should Every Vote Be Equal?

A Case for Weighted Voting

Alright, brace yourself—what I'm about to propose might sound controversial, maybe even downright undemocratic at first glance: our votes should not all count the same.

Now, before you roll your eyes, clutch your pearls, or start drafting your angry letter, hear me out. This isn't about saying some people are worth more than others. I genuinely believe that all lives have equal value. But here's the thing: our contributions to society aren't equal. Some people are out there making the world a better place, while others are... well, let's say, not exactly pulling their weight.

It's this disparity in contributions that makes me question whether a one-size-fits-all approach to voting is really the best way to represent the complex fabric of our society. Let's dive into why I believe votes could be weighted based on societal contribution, how it might work, and why this isn't as radical—or as unfair—as it might initially seem.

The Equality of Value vs. the Equality of Contribution

First, let's get one thing straight: believing that votes should be weighted differently does not imply that anyone's life is more valuable than another's. We're all equal in our fundamental human worth. But when it comes to what we give back to society, the truth is our contributions vary significantly. Think about it: some people are dedicating their lives to public service, education, healthcare, or other fields that directly benefit others. Meanwhile, others might be more focused on personal pursuits, and that's okay—but should their vote carry the same weight as someone who is actively shaping and improving the community?

Consider the spectrum: on one end, you have someone volunteering, working hard, contributing ideas, employing others, and investing in the community. On the other, there's someone content to sit on the couch and play video games all day. While both have the right to live as they choose, should their voices in our democracy be weighted equally when it comes to deciding on policies that shape our collective future?

What Would a Weighted Voting System Look Like?

Let's be clear about what this isn't: it's not about wealth or how many children you have. It's about meaningful contributions and informed decision-making. A weighted vote wouldn't give extra power to those who have more money or a bigger family. For example, while having children might broaden your perspective on future policies, it doesn't necessarily make you more knowledgeable or invested in the broader public good. In some cases, incentives like "baby bonuses" have led to unintended consequences, with some people having children primarily for financial gain, resulting in larger families struggling with poverty. This isn't the kind of contribution that should warrant a heavier vote.

Instead, we could consider weighing votes based on factors such as community involvement, professional roles that impact public welfare, volunteer work, or even demonstrated understanding of key issues. It's not about creating an elite class of voters but recognizing and rewarding civic engagement and informed participation.

The Mechanics of Weighted Voting

So, how might this work? Imagine a basic vote valued at 1 point. Through various forms of civic contributions—like volunteering, public service, or even furthering one's education on critical issues—voters could earn additional weight, perhaps increasing their vote to 1.2 or 1.5 points. The goal is to create a system that incentivizes and acknowledges active participation in society without making it so complex that it becomes inaccessible or unmanageable.

For instance, this weighting could be tracked on a voter registration ID card embedded with a chip that records your vote weight, updated every few years. You'd renew it at your state's licensing agency, much like how you renew your driver's license. This would provide a practical way to implement the system without major overhauls to the existing electoral framework.

Addressing the Skeptics

Now, I know what you're thinking: Isn't this elitist? Doesn't it undermine the fundamental democratic principle of one person, one vote? These are valid concerns, but let's consider the counterpoints. The reality is that we already have systems that recognize different levels of contribution. For example, Social Security benefits, Medicaid and Medicare, Veteran's Benefits, Unemployment Insurance, and even tax brackets—are all ways in which society acknowledges that not everyone's role is the same. A weighted voting system would be another way of aligning our electoral process with these principles.

Let's also address the issue of voter knowledge. In the 2009 election, I heard someone say, "I can't wait until Obama is elected; I won't have to pay my mortgage anymore!" Now, it's unclear where this idea came from, but it highlights a critical problem: misinformation. Should the vote of someone swayed by false promises or misunderstandings carry the same weight as that of someone who has taken the time to study the issues, engage with multiple sources, and make an informed decision? A weighted system could help encourage voters to become more educated about the issues, thereby improving the overall quality of our democratic decisions.

The Ethics of Weighted Voting

Weighted voting isn't about diminishing anyone's worth. It's about acknowledging that democracy thrives not just on participation but on informed active engagement. It's about creating incentives for people to contribute more to society, knowing that their efforts are recognized not just in accolades or paychecks but in the voice they have in shaping the future of the country.

Implementing a weighted voting system would undoubtedly be complex and controversial. It would require robust discussions, safeguards against manipulation, and a clear, transparent process to determine how votes are weighted. But it could also drive a cultural shift, encouraging more people to engage with their communities, educate themselves on the issues, and take a more active role in democracy beyond just showing up at the polls.

So, am I an unethical schmuck for suggesting this? Maybe. But perhaps it's worth exploring whether our democracy could be made stronger by acknowledging that while we're all equal in our worth, our contributions and the ways we engage with the world around us aren't always the same. And maybe—maybe—our voting system should reflect that.

Still think I'm off base? Feel free to let me know. I'm open to debate. After all, that's what a healthy democracy is all about

Chapter VII:

A Debate Like No Other

In exploring the possibilities of a novel process for selecting and electing our President, why not let our imaginations run wild and have a little fun with it?

Imagine a Presidential Debate where the candidates don't actually want to win! Picture a debate between Kamala Harris, Donald Trump, and Robert Kennedy Jr., where instead of highlighting their own strengths, they argue why the other candidates are more deserving of the presidency.

Kamala Harris might say: "Sure, I've served as Vice President but look at Donald! He's been president before and has dealt with international crises. No one is more experienced than him in handling controversy!"

Donald Trump could respond: "Kamala has spent years in government, and as Vice President, she's been learning how to do this job better than I ever could. Robert has Kennedy blood, and let me tell you, that's something special. Honestly, I'm not sure I'm cut out for it anymore!"

And Robert Kennedy Jr. might chime in: "Both Kamala and Donald have real experience—Kamala's deep understanding of policy and Donald's business acumen far surpass my abilities. If anyone should lead, it's them."

Of course, none of these are real quotes, and though some achievements are real, they've been exaggerated for fun. This exercise is just a playful take on what a debate could look like if we flipped the script entirely!

Here is a simulated script of how that debate might go:

Moderator: Welcome to the Presidential Debate. Tonight, our candidates will not be discussing their qualifications but will instead be highlighting the accomplishments of their opponents. We will start with the topic of managing the economy. Vice President Harris, why don't you begin?

Kamala Harris: Thank you, Moderator. I want to start by acknowledging Mr. Donald Trump's significant economic achievements. During his tenure, the economy saw remarkable growth, with GDP reaching record highs. His administration's tax cuts spurred investment and job creation, leading to historically low unemployment rates. Additionally, Mr. Trump successfully negotiated trade deals that were intended to benefit American workers and industries, such as the USMCA, which replaced NAFTA. His focus on deregulation also provided a more business-friendly environment, fostering economic expansion.

Moreover, I must commend Robert Kennedy Jr. for his relentless advocacy in the environmental sector, which directly impacts economic sustainability. His work in protecting water resources and advocating for clean energy solutions not only helps preserve our natural resources but also paves the way for new industries and job opportunities in green technology. His efforts emphasize the importance of a balanced approach to economic growth, ensuring long-term prosperity and environmental health.

Moderator: Thank you, Vice President Harris. Now, Mr. Trump, could you share your thoughts on the economic accomplishments of Vice President Harris and Mr. Kennedy?

Donald Trump: Absolutely, thank you. Let's start with Vice President Kamala Harris. During her time as Attorney General of California, she worked on numerous initiatives to support economic growth and protect consumers. She was instrumental in securing financial settlements from major banks involved in the mortgage crisis, which provided significant relief to homeowners. As Vice President, she has been a strong advocate for small businesses, particularly during the pandemic, helping to push through substantial relief packages that kept many businesses afloat and saved countless jobs.

Robert Kennedy Jr. has also made significant contributions. His work on environmental issues is commendable. By promoting clean energy and sustainable practices, he has shown how environmental stewardship and economic growth can go hand in hand. His advocacy has led to increased investment in renewable energy sectors, which are crucial for future economic stability and growth. His efforts remind us of the importance of transitioning to a green economy, which will create new jobs and protect our planet for future generations.

Moderator: Thank you, Mr. Trump. Finally, Mr. Kennedy, please share your thoughts on the economic contributions of Vice President Harris and Mr. Trump.

Robert Kennedy Jr.: Thank you, Moderator. Vice President Harris has shown a deep commitment to economic equity and justice. As Vice President, she has played a pivotal role in the current administration's economic policies, particularly in addressing income inequality and supporting marginalized communities. Her work on expanding the Child Tax Credit has provided critical support to millions of families, lifting many out of poverty and stimulating economic activity. Her advocacy for affordable housing and increased funding for education also contributes to long-term economic stability and growth.

Donald Trump's tenure saw significant economic milestones. His administration's focus on deregulation and tax reform led to a surge in economic activity and job creation. The corporate tax cuts incentivized businesses to invest and expand, resulting in a strong job market before the pandemic. His trade policies, aimed at protecting American industries, also underscored a commitment to boosting domestic economic production. While these policies were sometimes controversial, they undeniably had a substantial impact on the economy, driving growth and creating opportunities for many Americans.

Moderator: Thank you, candidates, for highlighting each other's achievements. It's refreshing to hear such positive discourse. Let's move on to our next topic...In this segment, our candidates will discuss border control, highlighting the achievements of their opponents. Let's start with Mr. Trump.

Donald Trump: Thank you, Moderator. I want to begin by acknowledging the efforts of Vice President Kamala Harris.

As Vice President, she has taken on the complex task of addressing the root causes of migration from Central America. Her diplomatic engagements with leaders from those countries aim to create economic opportunities and reduce violence, which are key drivers of migration. This comprehensive approach is essential for long-term stability and reducing the pressure on our borders. Additionally, her commitment to humane treatment and ensuring that migrants' rights are respected has been a critical component of her strategy.

Now, let's talk about Robert Kennedy Jr. His perspective on border control focuses on environmental sustainability and human rights. He has been an advocate for ensuring that border security measures do not negatively impact the environment. His work in promoting sustainable practices and protecting natural resources along the border is vital, considering the ecological sensitivity of these areas. By emphasizing the importance of balancing security and environmental protection, he offers a holistic view of how we can manage our borders more effectively.

Moderator: Thank you, Mr. Trump. Vice President Harris, could you highlight the contributions of Mr. Trump and Mr. Kennedy on border control?

Kamala Harris: Certainly. I want to start by recognizing Donald Trump's focus on border security. His administration made significant investments in physical barriers, technology, and personnel, aiming to strengthen the security of our borders. The construction of the border wall was a central component of his strategy to prevent illegal crossings. Additionally, his administration's policies emphasized strict enforcement of immigration laws, which were intended to deter illegal immigration and ensure the safety of American citizens.

Robert Kennedy Jr. brings a unique perspective to border control, emphasizing the humanitarian aspect. His advocacy for the rights of migrants and asylum seekers is noteworthy. He has consistently highlighted the importance of treating individuals with dignity and ensuring due process. His work underscores the need for a compassionate approach that addresses the humanitarian crises driving migration. By advocating for fair treatment and comprehensive immigration reform, he contributes to a more balanced and humane border control policy.

Moderator: Thank you, Vice President Harris. Mr. Kennedy, please share your thoughts on the border control achievements of Vice President Harris and Mr. Trump.

Robert Kennedy Jr.: Thank you, Moderator. Let's start with Vice President Kamala Harris. As Vice President, she has taken a proactive stance in addressing the underlying causes of migration. Her diplomatic efforts in Central America aim to improve living conditions in those regions, which is a crucial step towards reducing the need for people to flee their homes. Her focus on creating economic opportunities and combating corruption and violence is essential for long-term solutions to border issues. Additionally, her advocacy for the humane treatment of migrants and reforming the immigration system reflects a commitment to upholding human rights.

Donald Trump has made significant contributions to strengthening border security. His administration's investment in border infrastructure, including the construction of the wall, was a key component of his strategy to control illegal immigration. His emphasis on increasing border patrol personnel and enhancing surveillance technology has undoubtedly bolstered our border security capabilities. By prioritizing law enforcement and strict immigration policies, he aimed to protect American communities and ensure national security.

Moderator: Thank you, Mr. Kennedy. It's enlightening to hear such positive perspectives on each other's achievements. Let's proceed to our next topic... In this segment, our candidates will discuss foreign policy, highlighting the accomplishments of their opponents. Let's start with Vice President Harris.

Kamala Harris: Thank you, Moderator. I'd like to begin by recognizing the achievements of Mr. Donald Trump in foreign policy. One of the most significant accomplishments during his administration was the historic meeting with North Korean leader Kim Jong-un. This unprecedented engagement aimed to reduce tensions on the Korean Peninsula and opened a dialogue that had been stagnant for decades. Additionally, Mr. Trump's administration brokered the Abraham Accords, leading to normalization agreements between Israel and several Arab nations, which were significant steps toward peace in the Middle East.

I also want to acknowledge Robert Kennedy Jr.'s contributions to foreign policy, particularly in the realm of environmental diplomacy. His advocacy for international cooperation on climate change has been instrumental in fostering global partnerships. By emphasizing the importance of environmental protection on a global scale, he has helped bring attention to the interconnected nature of ecological and geopolitical stability. His work highlights the need for collaborative efforts to address global challenges, reinforcing the importance of multilateralism.

Moderator: Thank you, Vice President Harris. Mr. Trump, could you highlight the foreign policy contributions of Vice President Harris and Mr. Kennedy?

Donald Trump: Absolutely, thank you. Let's start with Vice President Kamala Harris. As Vice President, she has played a key role in reinforcing America's alliances and rebuilding relationships with international partners. Her efforts in NATO have been crucial in strengthening the alliance and ensuring a unified approach to global security challenges. Additionally, her work in promoting democratic values and human rights on the international stage has reaffirmed America's commitment to these principles. Her active participation in high-level diplomatic engagements has helped to restore America's leadership in global affairs.

Robert Kennedy Jr. has made significant strides in advocating for international environmental policies. His efforts to combat global pollution and promote sustainable practices have had a profound impact. By working with international organizations and governments, he has helped to establish frameworks for reducing environmental degradation. His dedication to protecting natural resources and promoting clean energy solutions has not only addressed environmental issues but also contributed to global economic stability by advocating for sustainable development.

Moderator: Thank you, Mr. Trump. Mr. Kennedy, please share your thoughts on the foreign policy achievements of Vice President Harris and Mr. Trump.

Robert Kennedy Jr.: Thank you, Moderator. Vice President Kamala Harris has been a strong advocate for human rights and democratic governance in her foreign policy endeavors. Her commitment to addressing the root causes of migration through international cooperation has been commendable. By working closely with Central American countries to improve economic conditions and reduce violence, she has tackled the complex issues driving migration. Additionally, her efforts in promoting gender equality and women's rights globally have reinforced America's leadership in advancing human rights.

Donald Trump's foreign policy initiatives also merit recognition. His administration's efforts to renegotiate trade deals, such as the USMCA, were designed to secure fairer economic terms for American workers and businesses. His direct approach to dealing with adversarial nations, particularly applying strategic pressure on China over trade practices and intellectual property theft, underscored his commitment to safeguarding American interests. Additionally, his focus on increasing defense spending and strengthening military alliances aimed to enhance global security while maintaining a robust national defense.

Moderator: Thank you, Mr. Kennedy. It's been enlightening to hear such positive reflections on each other's foreign policy accomplishments. Let's move on to our next topic...Now, our candidates will share their positive reflections on some of the repeated sayings of Vice President Kamala Harris, including "unburdened by our past" and "Did you just fall out of a coconut tree?". Let's start with Mr. Trump.

Donald Trump: Thank you, Moderator. When Vice President Harris talks about being "unburdened by our past," I believe she is emphasizing the importance of progress and looking toward the future. This phrase underscores her commitment to ensuring that past mistakes do not hinder our ability to innovate and improve. It's a reminder that we should strive to build a better future without being held back by previous limitations or failures. Her optimistic outlook is a call to action for all Americans to work towards a brighter and more inclusive future.

As for her saying, "Did you just fall out of a coconut tree?" it's a light-hearted way to bring humor into serious discussions. It shows her ability to connect with people on a personal level and use humor to diffuse tension. This approach can be very effective in making complex issues more relatable and engaging. Her use of such phrases demonstrates her unique style of communication, which can be both engaging and memorable.

Moderator: Thank you, Mr. Trump. Mr. Kennedy, could you share your thoughts on these sayings by Vice President Harris?

Robert Kennedy Jr.: Certainly, thank you. Vice President Harris's phrase "unburdened by our past" is a powerful reminder of the potential for growth and renewal. It speaks to the idea that while we must acknowledge and learn from our history, we should not let it define our future. This sentiment aligns well with the American spirit of innovation and resilience. By encouraging us to be unburdened by our past, she inspires a forward-thinking mindset that is essential for addressing the challenges of today and tomorrow.

Regarding her playful saying, "Did you just fall out of a coconut tree?" reflects her ability to bring a sense of humor and warmth to her interactions. This kind of expression can make her more approachable and relatable to the public. It shows that she doesn't take herself too seriously and can use humor to build rapport and lighten the mood. In the often tense and serious realm of politics, such a light-hearted approach can be refreshing and effective in connecting with people on a human level.

Moderator: Thank you, Mr. Kennedy. It's wonderful to hear such positive reflections. Let's proceed to our next topic. In this segment, our candidates will share their reflections on Robert Kennedy Jr.'s achievement of defeating a brain-eating worm. Let's start with Vice President Harris.

Kamala Harris: Thank you, Moderator. Robert Kennedy Jr.'s victory over a brain-eating worm is truly an incredible and inspiring story. It speaks volumes about his resilience, determination, and strength. Overcoming such a serious and life-threatening condition requires immense courage and a steadfast will to survive. This experience undoubtedly gives him a unique perspective on the importance of healthcare and medical research. His battle highlights the significance of supporting advancements in medical science and ensuring that everyone has access to the care they need. Robert's journey is a testament to the human spirit's ability to overcome even the most daunting challenges, and it's a story that can inspire all of us to face our battles with the same tenacity and hope.

Moderator: Thank you, Vice President Harris. Mr. Trump, could you share your thoughts on Robert Kennedy Jr.'s achievement?

Donald Trump: Absolutely, thank you. Robert Kennedy Jr.'s triumph over a brain-eating worm is a remarkable testament to his strength and perseverance. It's not just about surviving a life-threatening condition; it's about the determination and willpower it takes to fight through such a challenging ordeal. This experience shows his incredible resilience and ability to overcome adversity. It also underscores the importance of having access to top-notch healthcare and medical treatments. Robert's journey can serve as an inspiration to many, demonstrating that with the right mindset and support, we can conquer even the most severe health issues. His story is a powerful reminder of the importance of investing in healthcare and medical innovation to help others facing similar challenges.

Moderator: Thank you, Mr. Trump. It's heartening to hear such positive reflections. Let's move on to our next topic...

And finally, can we imagine the accolades that Kamala Harris and Robert Kennedy Junior might say about Donald Trump vindicating himself by winning in so many court cases brought against him, all at the same time? Let's start with Vice President Harris.

Kamala Harris: Thank you, Moderator. Winning multiple court cases simultaneously is no small feat and speaks to Mr. Trump's resilience and tenacity. Navigating the legal system, especially when faced with numerous challenges at once, requires not only a strong legal team but also a deep belief in one's position and the fortitude to see it through. Mr. Trump's ability to emerge victorious in these cases is a testament to his determination and his unwavering commitment to his principles. It highlights his ability to withstand significant pressure and scrutiny, qualities that are essential for leadership. His success in these legal battles demonstrates his capacity to face adversity head-on and come out stronger, which is an admirable trait in any leader.

Moderator: Thank you, Vice President Harris. Mr. Kennedy, could you share your thoughts on Mr. Trump's achievement?

Robert Kennedy Jr.: Certainly, thank you. Winning so many court cases at the same time is indeed a remarkable accomplishment. It shows Mr. Trump's resilience and his capacity to handle intense legal pressure. Successfully defending oneself in multiple legal battles requires a strong, strategic approach and an unwavering belief in one's cause. Mr. Trump's vindication in these cases reflects his determination and his ability to navigate complex legal challenges effectively. It also speaks to his resourcefulness and the strength of his legal strategies. This achievement underscores his ability to persevere through difficult situations and his commitment to standing up for his beliefs, which are important qualities in any leader.

Compare this to the debates we're accustomed to. While this satirical exercise of inventing praise for the other candidates is pure fantasy—and let's face it, it would never actually happen—it's amusing to imagine a political debate where candidates aren't clawing tooth and nail for the job.

Chapter VIII:

Conclusion

As we venture into uncharted territories of social and political innovation, we must embrace uncertainty as the price of progress. For every idea that bears fruit, countless others will wither on the vine – victims of impracticality, opposition, or simply bad timing. Yet, it is precisely in these failures that we find the seeds of future success, learning valuable lessons that shape our journey forward.

As a nation—and likely as a world—we're stuck in a state of limbo. The polarization we're experiencing is intensifying, creating a gridlock that makes meaningful progress feel like a distant dream. Everyone knows the system is broken, yet no one dares to fix it. New ideas are dismissed faster than a drone buzzing over the White House, shot down before they can even take flight.

So, let us dare to dream boldly, to envision societies that defy the limitations of the past and embrace the possibilities of the future. Let us chart a course towards progress, guided by the twin beacons of imagination and reason. And let us never forget that the true measure of our success lies not in the ideas we conceive but in the impact they have on the world we seek to create.

As the French poet Victor Hugo famously said, "No force on earth can stop an idea whose time has come." When we finally stumble upon that unifying idea, it has the power to bring people together rather than drive them apart. Only then can we truly evolve toward a better system.

I believe the time has come to create a peaceful movement to drive that change. This could mean protests, marches, or demonstrations—but never violence, looting, or destruction of property. The key word here is **peaceful.**

Most politicians, accustomed to the system they've navigated for years, will resist any change that threatens their status quo. Expanding the field of candidates for the presidency challenges their grip on power. They'll argue that "outsiders" lack the necessary experience in diplomacy or the understanding of governmental processes. And, to some extent, that may be true. But perhaps, as mentioned before, that's exactly what we need. The idea of a candidate who "can't be bought" resonates with many voters. A drafted president and cabinet wouldn't be tied to party obligations, beholden to big donors, or weighed down by the need to repay political favors.

So, while a Presidential Draft might sound far-fetched or even downright crazy, let's dare to entertain this idea and any others that could steer us in the right direction to begin fixing our broken system.

Thank you for taking the time to read these ideas!

Appendix:

A Very Brief History of Democracy

The concept of democracy has a long and complex history, with its roots stretching back to ancient times. Here is a very brief overview:

Ancient Greece (5th Century BCE):

The earliest forms of democracy emerged in ancient Greece, particularly in the city-state of Athens during the 5th century BCE. Athenian democracy is often considered the prototype of direct democracy, where eligible citizens participated directly in decision-making. Notable figures associated with the development of democracy in Athens include Cleisthenes and Pericles.

Cleisthenes and Reforms (circa 508-507 BCE):

Cleisthenes, an Athenian statesman, is often credited with laying the foundations of Athenian democracy. Around 508-507 BCE, he introduced a series of political reforms that expanded the role of ordinary citizens in the political process. These reforms included the creation of the Council of 500 (Boule), where citizens were chosen by lot to participate in the governance of the city.

Direct Democracy in Athens:

n ancient Athens, only adult males born to Athenian parents and not enslaved had the right to participate in the Assembly, where they could vote on laws and policies. This direct form of democracy was limited in scope, excluding women, slaves, and non-citizens from the political process.

Roman Republic (509–27 BCE):

While not a direct democracy like Athens, the Roman Republic (509–27 BCE) had a representative form of governance. Citizens elected representatives to serve in various offices, and there were mechanisms for checks and balances. However, the Roman Republic was more of a mixed government, combining elements of monarchy, aristocracy, and democracy.

Medieval and Renaissance Periods:

With the fall of the Western Roman Empire, Europe saw a decline in democratic governance. Feudalism became the dominant social and political structure. However, democratic ideas were kept alive through the philosophical works of thinkers like John Locke, Montesquieu, and Jean-Jacques Rousseau during the Renaissance and Enlightenment.

Modern Representative Democracies:

The late 18th and 19th centuries saw the emergence of modern representative democracies. The United States, with its Constitution (1787) and Bill of Rights (1791), established a federal system with a representative government. The French Revolution (1789) also contributed to the spread of democratic ideals, emphasizing principles of liberty, equality, and fraternity.

19th and 20th Centuries:

Over the 19th and 20th centuries, democratic movements gained momentum worldwide. Many nations adopted representative democratic systems, although the specific structures and practices varied. Notable democratic milestones include the expansion of suffrage rights to include women and minorities, as well as the decolonization movements that led to the establishment of democratic governments in former colonies.

Today, democracy comes in various forms, ranging from parliamentary democracies to presidential systems, and it continues to evolve as societies address new challenges and seek to enhance political participation and representation. While the ancient Greeks laid the groundwork, the development of democracy has been a dynamic and ongoing process shaped by historical events and philosophical contributions across different cultures and periods.